IMAGES OF
ITALY

Christmas 1991

" To The Losquadio's "

Love the
Ausco's

IMAGES OF
ITALY

ANNE GARROULD

INTRODUCED BY
JOHN JULIUS NORWICH

PYRAMID BOOKS

St Peter's and the Tiber The church stands on the site of Rome's largest cemetery where the body of St Peter the Apostle, martyred in either AD 64 or 67, was buried. His grave became a focal point for meetings of Christians and the earliest church dedicated to him was built in AD 324 by Constantine the Great.

By the 15th century, this structure had fallen into such a state of disrepair that the popes began to think about building a new church. In 1506, Pope Julius II ordered work to begin on its construction; Bramante, Raphael and Michelangelo were all involved in its design. The church as it is seen today was consecrated by Pope Urban VIII in 1626.

Page 1: **Local inhabitant, Prato**
Page 2: **San Maggiore, Venice**

First published in 1990
by Pyramid Books, an imprint of
The Octopus Publishing Group,
Michelin House, 81 Fulham Road, London SW3 6RB

ISBN 1-871-30781-3

Produced by Mandarin Offset
Printed and bound in Hong Kong

Introduction

We all of us, I suspect, have our own particular image of Italy: a memory, sometimes recent, sometimes recalled from the distant past, that seems to encapsulate everything about the country that we best know and love. My own dates back to the days soon after the Second World War, when my parents first took me – I must have been sixteen or so – to the Locanda di San Vigilio, a tiny hotel half-way along the eastern shore of Lake Garda. It was a small, unassertive, two-storey building, probably 16th-century, with a loggia running its entire length. To the north there was a terrace shaded by a huge chestnut tree, its outer wall – like that of the house itself – falling sheer to the lake, and beyond it a little chapel. To the south lay a shallow harbour for fishing boats.

As a hotel, it could never have been called comfortable. The beds were like concrete, there were no private bathrooms and in the public ones the plumbing was distinctly uncertain. But for beauty and tranquillity it knew no rival, and it possessed for us – though by no means for everyone – an additional advantage in the shape of its proprietor, a rascally and bibulous Irishman of considerable charm whose name was Walsh, but who was invariably known to his friends and the more privileged of his clients as Leonardo. His temper was mercurial and his conversation frequently crude; but his simple cooking – largely of fish drawn straight out of the lake – could not have been bettered, and as an inn-keeper there was, somewhere about him, a little touch of genius.

If you had a room overlooking the harbour – as I usually did – you would often awake on a summer morning to find it bathed from floor to ceiling in a brilliant orange glow, the sunshine being filtered through the immense sail of one of the boats that had come in a few hours before. Breakfast, lunch and dinner were eaten al fresco on the terrace – a crust of bread flung over the low wall at your elbow immediately summoning forth a hundred squabbling fish. Below you was the still and limpid water; opposite, in the distance, the little town of Sirmione, home of Catullus; while along to your right, if you craned your neck a little, you could see the ground rapidly rising towards Riva, at the northern end of the lake where, I liked to think, the Alps began. But the greatest reward of all was reserved for those who swam out fifty metres or so to a large, flat rock, clambered on to it as best they could (but gingerly, to avoid the limpets and barnacles) and then turned to face the shore. There stood San Vigilio in all its perfection – chapel and chestnut, house and harbour – while above and behind it a little olive grove climbed up the hillside to a line of cypresses along its crest.

One evening we drove to Verona for a performance of Romeo and Juliet, little dreaming that it was to be one of the most memorable theatrical experiences of our lives. It took place in the Piazza dei Signori – the most perfect setting imaginable – and the production did it full justice. At one moment we must have had over a hundred Montagues and Capulets brawling across the square, until a squadron of mounted cavalry thundered in to restore order; and there was another marvellous moment when Romeo leapt straight from the balcony on to his horse's back and galloped off on the road which, one knew perfectly well, did lead to Mantua.

Best of all was the end, when silent, hooded figures simultaneously appeared at every window of the square with blazing torches in their hands. That evening I knew that I was in love with Italy. I have remained so ever since.

I am fascinated, first of all, by the infinite variety of the place. It may in many ways have been a tragedy that Italy was so long in achieving unification; certainly the cost, in terms of human bloodshed, has been incalculable. But how great, too, has been the gain: in what other European country can you find a dozen or more cities outside the capital which are yet not remotely provincial in character, but which possess art and architecture of which any metropolis in the world would be proud – and, incidentally, self-confidence and swagger to match? Had the Roman Empire held, or had an Italian nation emerged, as did the French and English, in the Middle Ages, there would be no Venice or Florence as we know them today, no Turin or Milan, no Genoa or Pisa or Naples – just a lot of good, safe, stolid mercantile or manufacturing towns, utterly devoid of the panache that only independence can give.

Municipal braggadoccio is not, however, to be confused with individual style – an innate, instinctive visual responsiveness that sets the Italians apart from all other races. In the 14th and 15th-centuries, allied with a quite exceptional outburst of creative energy, it changed the course of European cultural history: but it is just as evident today – in clothes and cars and even computers, in the theatre of Giorgio Strehler and the films of Fellini and Visconti, in the Siena Palio and the operas performed in the Baths of Caracalla. On the personal level it hinges above all on the concept of the bella figura, *the necessity of cutting a dash; as such it adds infinite* amusement and colour to Italian life. One could wish, perhaps, that this same philosophy did not make it necessary for every young Italian to prove his voice, motor-bicycle or radio to be louder than anyone else's, and it may not be easy to convince yourself, when he revs up his Vespa under your hotel window at two o'clock in the morning to impress his girlfriend, that he is showing fundamentally the same qualities that gave rise to the Renaissance; but so, I believe, he is.

The Italians are not much given to subtlety or nuance; nor have they ever been particularly fond of abstract thought. Thus, although possessing one of the most exquisitely beautiful languages ever evolved by man, their literature remains in many respects surprisingly thin, and is still dominated by a writer – Dante – who has been dead for nearly seven centuries. Their taste is almost invariably for the visual, and where possible the spectacular. Painting, sculpture and architecture are the fields in which they excel; and though they have always been superb musicians, their greatest musical contribution has always been to the world of opera – where emotions are simple, straightforward and easily understood, and where there is something to look at as well as to listen to.

It seems hardly surprising therefore that, for most of us at least, our familiar images of Italy take on the same strong colours: azure sky, cobalt sea, golden sunshine, silver olives, green vines, red brick, white marble. Rome, Venice and Florence are surely the most theatrical cities in the world, the gondola the most romantic form of transport, St Peter's one of the most dramatic of churches. No country in Europe can boast more breathtaking scenery; and, with only three major active volcanoes on the entire continent, it is somehow typical of Italy to possess all three of them.

I began this introduction by recalling two specific images of Italy, as vivid in my memory today as they were forty years ago; and even while I have been writing it, hundreds more have come crowding into my mind. I have suddenly remembered, for example, the elderly violinist in the little trattoria behind the Pantheon in Rome, who from time to time would lay aside his fiddle and give astonishingly accurate telepathic answers to questions on scraps of paper scrunched up in the customers' fists; Padre Pio saying mass at 4am in the church of San Giovanni Rotondo, his hands covered with the little brown mittens he wore to conceal his stigmata; the wedding party among the stone monsters at Bomarzo, with the father of the bride bursting into tears half-way through his speech; the coronation of Pope Paul VI where, in the Borgia apartments of the Vatican, I drank the largest and most powerful dry martini of my life; the gondolier who fell into the Grand Canal, causing half a dozen of his colleagues to laugh so hard that they very nearly did the same; and the hitch-hiking Franciscan to whom I had given a lift, and whom, when he described the policemen who had just copped me for speeding as gli arcangeli della strada, *I could willingly have throttled. And yet, inexplicably, one of the clearest images of all is not visual but aural, still ringing in my ears after what must be well over a quarter of a century: the anguished cry of an exhausted American tourist in San Gimignano to his tireless companion:* 'What, more Ghirlandaio?'

John Julius Norwich

The Colosseum, Rome   This was begun by the Emperor Vespasian in AD 70 on the site of an artificial lake. Completed ten years later by his successor, Titus, the Colosseum held about 50,000 spectators: Gladiator fights, sea fights and drama were staged in the centre of the complex.

The Colosseum was originally called the Amphitheatrum Flavium and stood four storeys high above an oval ground plan. Its external structure has influenced architecture from the Renaissance onwards.

In Rome, more than in any other Italian city, one is conscious of the contrast between ancient and modern. The yellow bus in the foreground was built almost two millennia after the Colosseum.

The Arch of Titus, the Forum   This
stands at the beginning of the Via Sacra and
is decorated with relief scenes of Titus's
victory over the Jews at Jerusalem in AD 70.
It is a single-arched structure which was
built soon after his death in AD 81.

**The Temple of Antoninus and Faustina,
the Forum**   It was an Etruscan king,
Tarquinius Superbus, who drained the
marshy area between the Palatine and Capitoline Hills in about 510 BC. By the 5th
century AD the roughly rectangular area
had become a focal point for the religious
and political activities of the fast-growing
city.

The Temple of Antoninus and Faustina,
built in the 2nd century AD, occupied an
important place, standing just behind the
official residence of the Pontifex Maximus
and opposite the House of the Vestals.

The exterior of the Pantheon   The Emperor Agrippa built this round temple in 27 BC at the same time as his baths were being constructed. After a fire in AD 118 it was rebuilt by Hadrian. In AD 608 the temple was given to the Pope and thereafter became a church dedicated to all martyrs. Since the 16th century it has been a final resting place for eminent Italians and after 1870 members of the Italian royal family were buried here.

The interior of the Pantheon   The only source of light in the Pantheon is a round opening in the dome. The diameter of the temple exactly equals its height and its walls have two shells. The dome was originally gilded and the ceiling of the portico was covered with bronze. Like the Colosseum, the Pantheon has served as a model for countless other buildings from the 16th century onwards.

View over the Vatican   In addition to his private quarters in the Vatican, the Pope also has an official residence at Castel Gandolfo in the country south of Rome. There he can escape the heat of Roman summers.

St Peter's   Michelangelo based his design for the dome of St Peter's on that of Brunelleschi for the dome of the cathedral in Florence a century earlier. Marvelling at this dome, Michelangelo is reputed to have said:
Vado a Roma far la tua sorella
Di te più grande ma non di te più bella
(I'm going to Rome to construct your sister, larger than you but not more beautiful.)

Interior of St Peter's The amazing *baldacchino*, also by Bernini, immediately catches the eye. Its gilded twisting columns support the canopy above the papal altar and the afternoon sun enhances the dramatic effect of the great sunburst of rays emanating from the canopy. Bernini worked on this *baldacchino* from 1624 to 1628.

Behind the *baldacchino* is the throne of St Peter, again the work of Bernini. Together, the throne and the *baldacchino* symbolize the victory of the Christian church and also stand as a memorial to the genius of one of the greatest artists of the Baroque era.

St Peter's Bernini's masterly colonnades on either side of the façade of St Peter's symbolize the all-embracing arms of the Church. They also create a visible barrier between the Church and secular life but, since Bernini chose to construct colonnades rather than a solid wall, they do not divide the Church from that everyday life.

Castel Sant' Angelo   This was the burial place of the Emperor Hadrian who had reconstructed the Pantheon in the early years of the 2nd century as well as building a wall in northern Britain.

In the Middle Ages the castle passed into Papal hands and in the 13th century a passage – the Passetto – connecting it to the Vatican was constructed. This was particularly useful to Pope Clement VII in 1527; he fled from his quarters in the Vatican to the safety of the fortress when the French invaders stood at the gates of Rome. The castle remained in papal hands until 1901 serving as a refuge, a treasury and, in the renaissance, as a notorious prison.

Santa Maria in Aracoeli   This church, one of the 280 within the old city walls, was built by the Franciscans from 1250 onwards. It stands on the site of the Temple of Juno Moneta; beneath its fine Cosmatesque pavements lie Roman remains.

On 24 December, midnight mass is celebrated here. The church is crowded and the flickering candlelight only hints at the rich decoration. At the stroke of midnight 56 great chandeliers replace the candlelight with their brilliant illumination.

The steep staircase (devout pilgrims still climb it on their knees) leading to the church was commissioned in 1349 by the people of Rome in gratitude for Rome's deliverance from the plague – the Black Death – which had decimated cities to the north. According to tradition, the Tiburtine Sybil prophesied the coming of Christ to the Emperor Augustus where the church now stands.

Ponte Sant' Angelo and the Tiber (*preceding pages*)   Bernini conceived the climax of the Christian pilgrim's journey as beginning by the Ponte Sant' Angelo. The pilgrim would then walk along the Borgo Santo Spirito or pass, by a more circuitous route, through a crowded mediaeval quarter until he came to the Piazza San Pietro.

The wide boulevard along which the present-day visitor approached St Peter's was only built between 1936 and 1950. Its name, the Via della Conciliazione, commemorates the reconciliation between the Church and the State. One feels Bernini would have approved of the view it gives to visitors to St Peter's.

The Capitoline Square This lies between two peaks of the Capitoline Hill. Michelangelo designed the lay-out of the square, the Piazza del Campidoglio, in 1538, changing its orientation from the Forum and making it lead towards St Peter's (the commission for this work had come from Pope Paul III). The Musei Capitolini stay open late on Saturday evenings and so, especially in summer, the Piazza del Campidoglio becomes a meeting place for the Romans.

Piazza Venezia, Rome The inhabitants of Rome often refer to the monument to Victor Emmanuel II as 'the typewriter'. Built by Sacconi during the years 1885—1911, it necessitated the destruction of two earlier palaces. It resembles a sacrificial altar; perhaps this was an intentional allusion on Sacconi's part since nearby lies the Foro Traiano with its echoes of pagan times.

In front of the monument, on a pedestal, is the Altare della Patria, its eternal flame guarded by two soldiers. The equestrian statue is that of United Italy's first king, Victor Emmanuel II.

Detail of fountain in Piazza Farnese
Two enormous baths, originally in the Terme di Caracalla, have been converted into fountains. Water in Rome is all-important; every night some streets are hosed clean. The authorities work a weekly rota, dividing the city into sectors which can be cleaned during the hours of darkness.

Fountain in Piazza Navona   In the first century AD the Stadium of Domitian stood on this site. By the end of the 15th century the Piazza was of considerable importance in everyday life in Rome since the Capitoline market had been transferred here in 1447. Games and festivals are still held here and at Christmas there is an outdoor market where decorations, toys and sweets can be bought. The Piazza did not reach its final Baroque form until the mid-1650s. In 1648 Pope Innocent X (a member of the Pamphilj family who owned a large *palazzo* on the Piazza) commissioned the Fontana dei Fiumi from Bernini. The figures were carved by Bernini's assistants and represent four major rivers of the world – the Danube, the Nile, the Ganges and the Plate. Pope Innocent insisted upon the inclusion of the obelisk as a symbol of the Church's triumph.

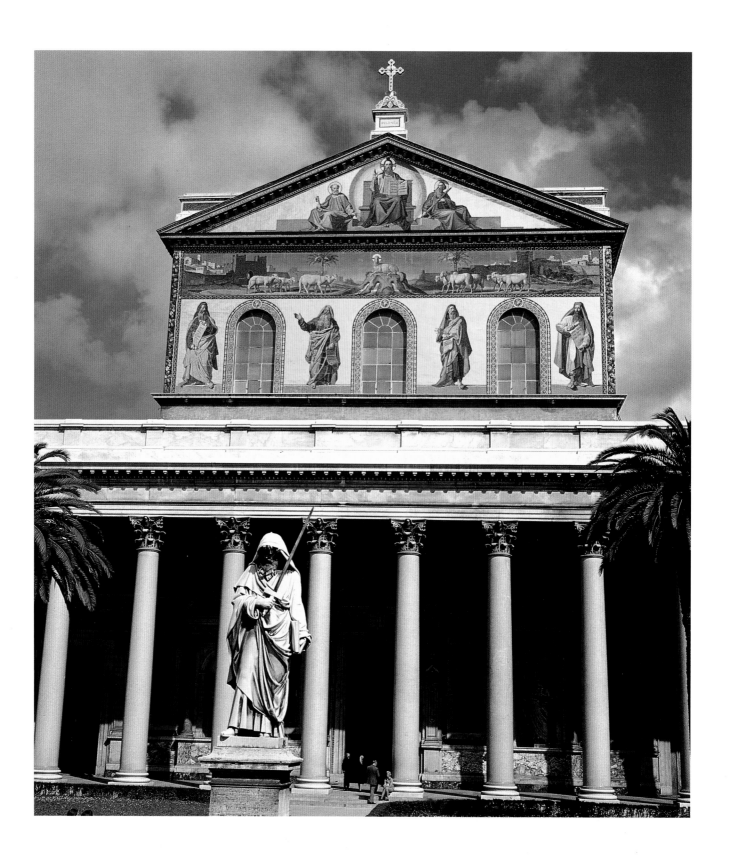

San Paolo fuori le Mura   The church of St Paul-outside-the-walls is the third of the *basilicae maiores* – basilicas were the first large buildings constructed specifically for religious purposes. It was built in AD 386 over the spot where St Paul was said to have been buried in AD 67. The 5th-century church which replaced the earlier one was itself much altered before being almost totally destroyed in a fire in 1823. The present-day church is a reconstruction dating from 1854. The architect, Poletti, based his plans on those of an early Christian basilica.

In the mosaics in the apse, Christ sits in majesty between St Peter, St Paul and St Andrew. St Peter, readily identifiable by the two keys he holds, stands on Christ's left whilst St Paul is to the right. Barely visible to the naked eye, the tiny figure of Pope Honorius III kneels to kiss the right foot of Christ.

Café in the Piazza Campo dei Fiori
Cafés feature prominently in the lives of most Italians. In the early mornings men can be seen standing at the bars of small cafés, drinking an *espresso* before starting their day's work. Quite often the *espresso* is accompanied by an *aperitivo* or a glass of wine. In the middle of the morning the café population will be increased by an influx of tourists. The photographer has captured a rare moment of tranquillity in the normally bustling café scene.

Eating out is far more commonplace in Italy than in Great Britain, since restaurants are places for meeting friends. The choice is extensive and prices can range from exorbitant to amazingly cheap. A usually reliable test is to enter a restaurant and stand listening to the converstion. If it is predominantly in Italian, stay. If not, find somewhere else. Restaurants advertising a *Menu turistico* are usually best avoided.

Via Appia Appius Caecus, a censor, built the Via Appia in 312 BC . The road, leading south to Brindisi, still bears witness to the type of traffic which used it – the narrow channels in many of the stones were made by the iron wheels of chariots.

Since the ancient Romans were not allowed to bury their dead within the city walls, many of the major roads leading out of Rome were used as burial grounds. The oldest tomb monument in Rome – the Tomb of the Scipios – is in the first section of the Via Appia, just by the Porta San Sebastiano.

The Greek temple of Neptune   Paestum lies in Magna Graecia, the name given to that part of Italy settled by Greeks from Sybaris around 600 BC . Originally called Poseidonia (after Poseidon, the Greek god of the sea), it fell into the hands of the Lucananian tribe in the 4th century BC and then came under Roman domination. The ruined temple of Neptune (the Roman god of the sea) was actually dedicated to Hera Argiva. Built around 460–450 BC , in classical Doric style, it is an eloquent reminder of the beauty and power of Greek architecture. It antedates the Parthenon in Athens by only a few years.

The Doric columns of the temple were carved in travertine marble of which there are still deposits not far from Rome. However, after almost 2500 years, the travertine is showing some signs of erosion.

Fishing boats, Pozzuoli   The elliptical curves of these fishing boats in the inner harbour at Pozzuoli seem to echo the curve of the amphitheatre.

Flavian amphitheatre, Pozzuoli   Samian Greeks founded the colony of Dikaearchia in the 6th century BC. In 194 BC it became a Roman colony, Puteoli, and developed into an important port. It was left virtually in ruins as a result of the barbarian invasions in the Middle Ages. The Flavian Amphitheatre was built during the reign of the Emperor Vespasian (AD 69–79) and was designed as a place where sea battles could be staged. Capable of holding some 35,000 spectators, it was the third largest amphitheatre of classical times, Rome and Capua being larger. The other walls have virtually disappeared, the stones having been re-used in later buildings.

Wall painting, Pompeii Many of the houses had splendid façades and richly decorated interiors which bore witness to the owners' wealth. The wall paintings, equally well-preserved by the exclusion of air, are of landscapes, flying swans, scenes from the Trojan war or mythological subjects. The wall paintings from the private rooms of the 'House of Julia Felix' are now in the Louvre.

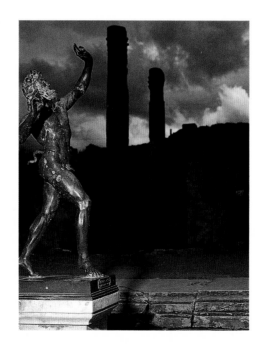

Herculaneum Unlike the inhabitants of Pompeii, those of Ercolano (Herculaneum) had advance warning of the eruption. The molten lava from Vesuvius cooled into a solid mass preserving the buildings and their decorations. Although excavations began in the 18th century, it is only since the early years of the 20th century that these have been pursued in accordance with any system; the actual site of Ercolano now lies below the modern town of Resina. However, excavations have uncovered rows of multi-storeyed houses, reminiscent of those found in Ostia.

Pompeii and Mount Vesuvius A dramatic photograph of the volcano which erupted and buried Pompeii, Herculaneum and Stabiae on 24 August, AD 79. Pompeii was covered with ash, pumice and sulphur to a depth of 7 metres. Systematically excavated since 1869, 60 per cent of the Roman town has been uncovered.

Mosaic of Neptune and Amphitrite, Herculaneum One of the best-preserved interiors in Herculaneum. The mosaic was found in surprisingly good condition. The ruins of Herculaneum were discovered by pure chance when a well-shaft was sunk in 1709.

An interior, Herculaneum The rich inhabitants could afford to decorate the interiors of their houses with wall paintings and sculpture. The naked male figure would seem to be the work of a very competent sculptor. Some of the decorative floor tiles have also survived.

Trulli houses, Alberobello One entire section of this Apulian town, containing about a thousand habitations, is built in the *trulli* style. Alberobello was founded in the 17th century at a time when the King of the Two Sicilies levied taxes from all new towns. In order to avoid paying these taxes, the inhabitants developed a style of architecture which allowed them to pull down the houses as soon as they got wind of an imminent visit from the royal tax collectors. When the officials had departed, the houses would be rebuilt.

The Alberobellini were, in fact, reverting to an ancient style of building in which the conical roof is layered like a dummy vault, without using mortar. Each stone juts out above the one below. The inhabitants continued to build in this manner even when Murat, King of Naples, officially recognized the new town and legalized the use of mortar.

The Cathedral, Amalfi Around AD 1000, Amalfi was one of Italy's most eminent maritime trading republics. The *Tavole Amalfitane*, used as the maritime laws at that time, are preserved in the local museum. In 1073 the Normans conquered Amalfi; in 1135 it was plundered by the sailors from one of its rival sea-ports, Pisa. According to tradition, Amalfi was the home of Flavio Gioia who invented the compass.

The Cathedral was rebuilt around 1200 and has also been altered many times since then. The splendid bronze door of the main portal was executed in Constantinople by a certain Master Simon in the year 1066 when the Normans were occupied elsewhere. Master Simon's door has survived from the earlier 9th-century building.

Abruzzi shepherd playing carols One Christmas in Rome a *presepio* was set up on the main landing half-way up the Spanish Steps. Nearby stood a shepherd from the Abruzzi mountains, clad in garments similar to the shepherds shown in the *presepio*. While he played somewhat mournful carols on his bagpipes, small children watched and listened, wide-eyed and entranced.

Crib, Naples At Christmas, many Catholic churches in Italy display elaborate panoramic models of the Nativity. Often these *presepi* have been preserved for generations and are a source of considerable pride for individual churches. The most elaborate *presepi* are those created in Naples in the 18th century. Great attention was paid to detail – costume, naturalistic effects and lighting were of paramount importance.

Fireworks over Calabria Natural and man-made pyrotechnics. Often at the end of Ferragosto (strictly speaking only 15 August, but used loosely to refer to a holiday period in August), the Italians organize magnificent firework displays which are elaborately and imaginatively choreographed.

Mount Etna, Sicily   The island of Sicily enjoys a wonderful climate, an enviably central trading position and great agricultural wealth; it also suffers from earthquakes. This disadvantage has never outweighed the advantages since in its history Sicily has been fought over by Greeks, Phoenicians, Romans, Goths, Byzantines, Saracens, Normans, Germans, Frenchmen and Spaniards until finally, in 1861, it became part of the Kingdom of Italy.

Sicily produces cereals, wine, olives and citrus fruit. *Tarocchi*, the purple-red blood oranges, have a short four to six week season in February and March; they are to be found in the markets in Northern Italy several weeks before fruit grown on the mainland is ready for marketing.

Monreale Cathedral, Sicily The town of Monreale, which grew up around its splendid cathedral, lies at the foot of Monte Caputo. Situated high up on a hill overlooking Palermo, the capital of Sicily, the cathedral is one of the outstanding Romanesque buildings in Italy. Founded in 1174 by William II of Sicily (nicknamed 'the Good') it is constructed of pale, rather chalky tufa and black lava.

Workers came from all over Italy to decorate the new building. Bonanno travelled from Pisa where he had been responsible for the bronze Portale di San Ranieri of the cathedral to make two bronze doors for the main façade of Monreale; mosaicists came from Venice to decorate the interior. The names of the architect or architects have not been recorded but the interlaced pointed blind arcades and the magnificent cloister bear witness to his (or their) imagination and ability.

Interior of Monreale Cathedral The sumptuous decoration of the interior spans many centuries. Sicilian mosaicists were employed to help the Venetians; they completed the mosaic decoration in 1182, depicting scenes from the Old and New Testaments. The pavement, which is original, is made of marble, granite and porphyry. The founder of the cathedral, William the Good, is not only buried here; he is also portrayed in a mosaic near the sanctuary, being crowned by Jesus Christ.

Cheeses, Reggio di Calabria   Italy produces many kinds of cheese; some of the lesser-known regional cheeses are extremely good.

Reggio di Calabria was founded around 720 BC by Greeks from Chalcis. The *objets d'art* and artefacts they brought with them to embellish their surroundings together with work created in Reggio, are to be found in the Archaeological Museum. The city itself was virtually destroyed by an earthquake in 1908.

Delivering fruit, Sardinia   For many years Sardinia has lagged far behind the rest of Italy in keeping up with the advances of technology. The introduction of the small three-wheeled delivery van has made life much easier for tradesmen, builders and the like.

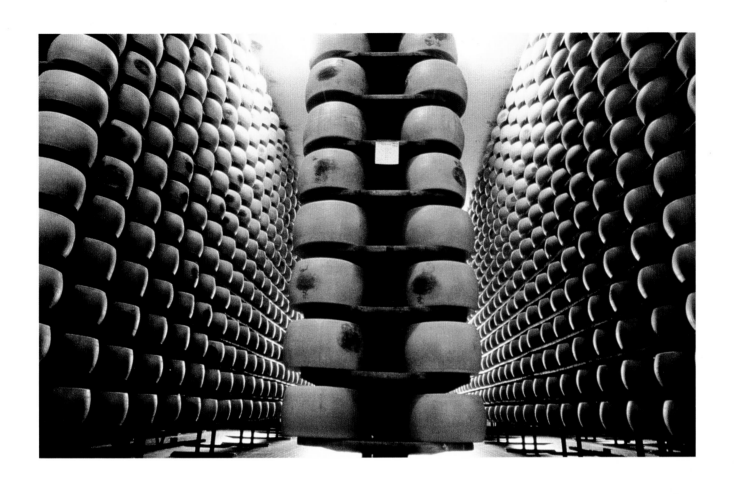

Wine-tasting, Elba Virgil praised Elba not for its wine but for the quality of its high-grade ores. Even before Virgil, the Etruscans had discovered these ores and worked them in the furnaces of Porto Baratti. The main town of Elba is called Portoferraio (iron port). Napoleon had three villas on the island. When he abdicated in 1815, Elba became part of the Grand Duchy of Tuscany. Here it will cost the passer-by nothing to sample the local wines.

Wine cart, Ischia The island of Ischia, which is volcanic in origin, was the first place in Italy to be settled by Greeks in the 8th century BC. Its major buildings date from the 14th and 15th centuries, the period of its affluence. In the 19th century it was discovered that its radioactive mineral springs were beneficial to sufferers from gout and rheumatism. However, over-indulgence in the local wine could counter-act the effect of the spring water.

Storm over Lake Maggiore This is the
second largest lake in Italy, although about
one-fifth of it at the northern end actually
belongs to Switzerland. The rivers and tri-
butaries which flow into Lake Maggiore are
fed by melting snow from the Alps so it is
subject to sudden floods.

Fearsome and unexpected storms are
caused by the wind called the *Maggiora*.
Winds blow across the lake from all points
of the compass. Until about 10am, the
Tramontana blows from the north; after
this time the wind shifts to the south and
becomes the *Inverna*. The westerly wind is
called the *Mergozzo*.

Isola Bella from a ferry Ferries regularly
ply up and down Lake Maggiore. In summer there are also hydrofoils that carry
passengers between Stresa and Locarno.

Bellagio, Lake Como   Known for its silk-weaving and olive-wood carving, Bellagio is a delightful old Lombard town. It is situated on a headland where Lake Como divides – the western arm is a continuation of the main lake whereas the eastern arm is called Lago di Lecco.

Virgil's name for this lake was *Lacus Larius* from which its alternative name of Lago Lario is derived.

Basilica, Isola San Giulio, Lake Orta The island lies on Lake Orta, one of the less-visited lakes in Piedmont. The steamboat from Orta takes only five minutes to reach the Isola San Giulio which was once uninhabited because of its large population of snakes and other less-prepossessing forms of wildlife. In AD 390 St Julius, the founder of this church, is said to have freed the island from these unwelcome pests.

The Basilica dates from the 11th century but, as with so many churches in Italy, was added to over the centuries. Its present form is 18th-century Baroque. In the sacristy is a whale's vertebra representing a bone of one of the serpents St Julius destroyed.

Nowadays, the wealthy Milanese aristocracy have their villas on the island.

Calm waters, Lake Garda The Romans called Lake Garda, the largest of the Italian lakes, *Lacus Benacus*. Wildfowl come here in their thousands. Fish are still plentiful, despite the fact that their numbers have been depleted by netting. Two winds predominate on this lake; in the morning the *Sover* blows from the north whilst in the afternoon it is the *Ora* from the south. Both winds can whip up the waters into violent storms.

Morning sun over the Italian Alps
Hannibal must surely have followed similar
valleys during his six-month crossing of the
Alps. He finally led his troops into the
fertile area surrounding the river Po in
September 218 BC.

Alpine village of Livigno The long straggling village of Livigno is now a ski resort much frequented by the Milanese.

In springtime, melting snow from the Alps and the Dolomites can cause considerable problems, flooding rivers and valleys in the Po plain.

The Matterhorn seen from Breuil-Cervinia The Matterhorn is almost 4500 metres high. Most of the earliest attempts to scale it were made from Breuil-Cervinia but the mountain was not climbed from this side until 1867. Originally the town was known only as Breuil; in the 1920s it was given the additional name of Cervinia from the French and Italian names for the mountain – Mont Cervin and Monte Cervino. The mountain guides of Breuil-Cervinia are particularly sought after.

The Cathedral, Milan Dedicated to the Nativity of the Virgin, Milan's cathedral is the most magnificent Gothic building in northern Italy. In size in Italy it is second only to St Peter's in Rome. It was begun about 1386; between 1765 and 1769 the topmost spires were added but the façade was not completed until 1813. The central spire is capped by a statue of the Madonna – La Madonnina – 108 metres above the ground. The statue is of gilded copper and is almost four metres in height. No other building in Milan may rise higher.

It was in Milan Cathedral in 1805 that Napoleon crowned himself King of Italy with the Iron Crown.

Above The astonishing intricacy of the carving can be appreciated in this photograph.

Galleria Vittorio Emanuele II, Milan The building of this Galleria, together with the redesigning of the Piazza del Duomo (Cathedral Square) completely changed the centre of Milan. The Galleria was constructed between 1865 and 1877 to house an arcade of shops between the Piazza del Duomo and the Piazza della Scala. Cruciform in plan, with an iron and glass roof, it is decorated with mosaics symbolizing the four continents, the arts, science, agriculture and industry.

The Galleria as a whole was intended as a monument to the new State – hence its dedication to the first King of United Italy and its siting, as both a political and a moral symbol, so close to the Cathedral. Guiseppe Mengoni, its designer, would not have appreciated the inclusion, in 1989, of a Macdonald's Fast Food shop almost directly below the central cupola.

Sunflowers growing in Tuscany   Sunflowers are a commercial crop in Italy, grown particularly for their oil, which is now much in demand. The heads of the flowers always turn towards the sun, following its daily passage from east to west. When the flowers begin to die in late summer, the heads droop and show only the much paler underside. Harvesting takes place when the heads have dried off and are completely brown.

Delivering provisions, Ovada   This village lies to the north-west of Genoa at the head of a valley. Provisions have to be delivered by cable since the mountain side is so steep.

Emilia Romagna This region covers a sizeable area, stretching from the middle and lower Po in the north, to the Apennines in the west and to the Adriatic in the east. Bologna is the chief town. The climate is immensely varied; winters can be extremely cold and summers stiflingly hot. Spring and autumn are the best seasons in which to visit Emilia Romagna. In spring one can see the delicate new green leaves just as Pinturicchio painted them in the early 16th century. In autumn the trees along the Via Emilia (the great Roman road which gave its name to the region) are ablaze with crimson and russet and gold.

Tuscan farmhouses Many such buildings have been bought as country residences, either by wealthy Italians or by foreigners. In the 1950s and 1960s the children of the *contadini* who owned these houses left home to seek their fortunes in Rome, Milan or Turin. When their parents died the properties fell into disrepair and nature reclaimed the land. A generation later, both are being restored, thanks to the efforts of their new owners who often rise at 5am to help spray the vines or prune the olive trees.

Overleaf Vines and olive-trees were much damaged in the winter of 1985 when four nights of severe frost occurred. Each region has its own distinctive wine. Chianti is a district particularly renowned for red wines.

View of San Gimignano Until about 20 years ago, San Gimignano was something of a time-capsule. Once the site of an Etruscan settlement dating from the 3rd or 4th centuries BC , San Gimignano became a flourishing town encircled by 13th-century walls. Thirteen of the towers which gave it its full name, San Gimignano delle belle Torri, still exist. No one knows exactly how many towers were built originally; estimates vary between 56 and 76.

The mediaeval appearance of the town has been preserved although over the last few years concessions have been made to the growing tourist industry. This has resulted in artisans' shops – unsophisticated, poorly-lit and full of intriguing long-forgotten treasures – being replaced by boutiques with shining plate-glass windows behind which the latest Florence fashions are displayed under garish lighting.

Parade of banners, Corsa del Palio, Siena
Not only do the jockeys involved in the
race wear mediaeval costume in the colours of the *contrada* they represent but all
the others who take part in the parade are
similarly dressed. The long and colourful
parade before the race includes displays of
sbandierata (banner-throwing). The *alfieri*
or flag-throwers begin when very young,
imitating the adults. Later they attend a
course organized annually by each
contrada. Between 80 and 100 of the best
alfieri then perform in the Palio.

Palazzo Pubblico and Il Campo, Siena

The name of Siena is inextricably linked with the Palio which is always referred to, incorrectly, as a horse race. In fact the Palio is a banner for which the Corsa del Palio is run. Ten jockeys riding bareback race three times round Il Campo which is specially prepared for the event. The winner of the Palio is the first horse home; it matters not if the jockey has parted company with his mount.

The ten horses represent ten of the seventeen *contrade* or districts into which Siena is divided. Lots are drawn for which *contrade* shall be represented in the race held on 2 July (the Visitation – a Roman Catholic festival). The seven *contrade* not selected for that day are guaranteed a place in the second Corsa del Palio which takes place on 16 August, the day after the Assumption of the Virgin. Again, lots are drawn to decide the other three contestants.

The Palazzo Pubblico, built in the Sienese Gothic style, dates from 1297 to 1310 and was once the seat of the Signoria and the Podestà, the men who governed Siena. Between 1338 and 1348 the Rinaldo brothers built the Torre del Mangia, the tall belltower to the left of the Palazzo.

Corsa del Palio, Siena Excitement is at fever pitch before the start of the race. The centre of the Campo holds up to 80,000 people; those who faint are passed over the heads of the other spectators to first-aid posts at the edge of the Campo.

The jockeys battle for position at the start since the first horse away is usually the winner. Bribes of millions of lire change hands, even seconds before the start of the race since the *contrade* who know that they have drawn a poor or an unknown horse will do all they can to prevent the horses of their greatest rivals winning.

The jockeys are not Sienese; they are usually Sardinians hired by the *contrade* for large sums of money. Losing jockeys need to be good runners – unless they get away and disappear immediately after the race, they will, in all probability, be quite severely beaten up.

The Campo is fan-shaped and stands on the site of the original forum. There are two legends about the founding of Siena; one has it that Siena was founded by the Senones (Gauls), another that it was established by Senio, the son of Remus. Certainly Siena existed in Etruscan times. Under Augustus it was a Roman colony known as Saena Julia.

Left A drummer in the costume of the Civetta (owl) *contrada*. Other *contrade* are named after the dragon, the wave and the tower. The last two are bitter rivals.

Sienese speciality *Panforte* (literally 'strong bread') is a speciality of Siena. Basically it is a flat circular cake containing dried fruit and various types of nuts. Chocolate or pepper can be added to the mixture – the *peperone* is an acquired taste. In Siena there are two major companies which produce *panforte* – Nannini and Sapori.

The Cathedral, Siena Dedicated to the Assumption of the Virgin, the Cathedral was begun in 1196 and virtually finished by 1215. To decorate its façade the Sienese sought a sculptor from Pisa since there was no real tradition of sculpture in Siena. Giovanni Pisano and his father Nicola carved the pulpit in the Cathedral, finishing it in 1268. Thereafter Giovanni worked alone on the sculptures of the façade, producing some of the most astoundingly modern and intensely moving figures of the 13th century.

View of Palazzo Ducale, Urbino

Although Urbino can trace its history back to the Umbrian leader, Metaurus Suassus, who lived some two centuries before Christ, it owes its real glory to Federigo da Montefeltro, a mercenary soldier who created around him, between 1444 and 1482, a court and indeed a way of living which were widely admired in the rest of western Europe. To build his palace, Federigo employed Luciano Laurana, an architect from Dalmatia, who produced one of the most elegant and satisfying structures in northern Italy.

It was here that the eight-year-old Raphael came daily with his father who was employed by Federigo and it was on this court and its *modus vivendi* that Baldassare Castiglione based his book *The Courtier*. Our debt to Federigo, the illegitimate son of the Count of Montefeltro, is indeed great.

Basilica di San Francesco, Assisi St
Francis founded his Order on a rule of
poverty, chastity and obedience. Less than
40 years after his death, Pope Innocent IV,
in 1253, consecrated one of the most richly
adorned churches in Italy to the memory of
this gentle saint. Cimabue, Giotto and
Simone Martini decorated the walls;
Cavallini came from Rome to paint a series
of 32 frescoes of scenes from the Old
Testament; workers in marble and stained
glass added to the wealth of its embellish-
ment. St Francis would have been
astonished and, perhaps, a little dismayed.

Roofscape in Assisi The town is not only
on the side of a hill, its streets also cross
dried-out gullies so that one is constantly
walking up- or downhill. All new buildings
must be constructed from the yellowish-
grey stone used in the mediaeval buildings
so there is a strong sense of unity in the
architecture in Assisi.

Hermitage on Monte Subasio, Assisi

This hermitage, set in dense wood some five kilometres from Assisi, was built in the 18th century to commemorate the spot where St Francis used to come and meditate. St Francis, who was born in 1186, was the son of a rich merchant who traded in France and preferred to call his son Francesco rather than by his baptismal name Giovanni.

The boy's youth was somewhat wild – he was imprisoned in Perugia for one year. After this term of imprisonment he was struck down by an illness and his thoughts turned to the religious life. He died in October 1226.

The ice-cream seller The ubiquitous three-wheeler van has been converted to carry a deep freeze. During the winter months this man will probably return to the country to look after his smallholding.

Cheeses in a Bologna shop There are almost as many varieties of cheese in Italy as there are of pasta. Depending on the region, the cheese may be made from the milk of goats, sheep or cows. One of the largest producers of milk in Italy is the company called Parmalat; its trade name is a combination of the name of the chief city in the milk-producing area and part of the Italian word *latte* (milk).

Sweet specialities The Italian word *dolci* is used to describe desserts such as tarts made with almonds or a mixture of fruits. Sweets or candies are called *caramelli* and again many regions have their speciality. Perugia boasts the *baci di Perugia* (kisses of Perugia) which are whirls of milk chocolate with a soft centre and a single hazelnut.

Football match *Il calcio* is a national sport. Even in the heat of summer young men practise their goal-shots, hoping to be chosen one day to play for Lazio (the Rome team), Juventus or AC Milan. Any patch of waste ground can become a football pitch.

A street in Spoleto The 20th-century painter Giorgio di Chirico painted metaphysical paintings, one of which was called *The Melancholy of the Street*. Like this photograph, the painting depicts an empty street with strongly contrasted areas of light and shade.

Street sweeper, Spoleto Italian cities and towns are normally kept very clean. The Comune (Town Council) takes great pride in presenting the most pleasant aspect of its town to visitors. In Lucca, for example, there was a formal flower-bed showing the date in flowers – obviously this had to be tended daily.

The Cathedral, Spoleto The Festival of Two Worlds, largely inspired by the composer Giancarlo Menotti, is held here each year from 15 June to 15 July. Concerts take place in the Cathedral Square, sculpture is displayed around the town and films and theatrical performances are given in the Roman theatre and the deconsecrated Church of San Niccolo.

The Cathedral, consecrated in 1198, has been much altered. Inside are delightful frescoes by Pinturicchio and Filippo Lippi. The countryside around Spoleto is very beautiful and clearly left its mark on these two artists.

The Cathedral, Orvieto One of the largest cities in Umbria, Orvieto is built on a tufa crag. Etruscans settled here centuries before the birth of Christ. The Cathedral, of which the façade dates from 1308 to 1330, is architecturally unique; the interior has frescoes by Fra Angelico and Luca Signorelli.

Orvieto can also be said to have three other claims to fame: its wine, its pottery and its lace. The Orvietane (women of Orvieto) used to sit out of doors, working on most delicate and intricate patterns. Lace bedspreads cost a fortune; tablecloths are a little less expensive. In each case one can imagine the finished article becoming a family heirloom.

The outskirts of Cassara This pictures-
que town lies near the coast of the Gulf of
Genoa. In the Cathedral Square is a house
where Michelangelo is believed to have
stayed during his visits to the nearby quarries to purchase marble. The port for ship-
ping marble to all parts of the world is at
Marina di Carrara some three kilometres
from the town itself.

Blocks of marble near Carrara   Blocks of marble weighing between 30 and 60 tonnes are transported down narrow, un-made-up mountain roads on huge trailers. It is disconcerting to meet such a trailer when driving a mere car uphill to visit the quarries.

Marble quarries, Colonnata   There are six buses a day between Carrara and the marble quarries at Colonnata in the Apuan Alps. These quarries have been worked for over two thousand years. It was from one called *Bianco di Bianco* (whitest of white) that Michelangelo sought the marble for his first *Pietà* – the Virgin with the dead Christ on her lap, now in St Peter's in Rome.

What might be mistaken for snow on the mountainside is actually marble; in the course of cutting it, small rivers of marble chips slide down the mountainside.

Façade of San Michele in Foro, Lucca This church, begun about 1143, stands on the site of the Roman forum. The fantasy and imagination of the architects seem to herald the style of Antonio Gaudi and his Church of the Holy Family in Barcelona, built more than eight centuries later. The wings of the Archangel Michael are specially constructed to allow the wind to pass through them.

Roman amphitheatre, Lucca One of the most enchanting towns in Tuscany, Lucca has many Roman remains. The walls of the mediaeval houses around the elliptical amphitheatre incorporate some of the massive stones used in its construction in the 2nd century AD. Sometimes in spring there is a horticultural show in the amphitheatre; the azaleas, camellias and rhododendrons are a profusion of colour.

Via del Fosso, Lucca *Il fosso* means 'the ditch'. This street is probably the widest in the old part of Lucca which is characterized by narrow streets without pavements. Unlike some cities – Siena, for example – the centre of Lucca is not closed to traffic. Windowsills on the ground floor of palaces jut out into the street so being a pedestrian can, on occasions, be somewhat hazardous.

Piazza dei Miracoli, Pisa One's first view of Pisa should be from the gate at the south-west corner of the Piazza dei Miracoli. The four great white marble buildings, seen in brilliant sunlight in their setting of green lawns, leave a lasting impression on even the most seasoned of travellers. Of the four buildings, the Cathedral is the oldest, having been begun in 1063.

Lungarno, with Santa Maria della Spina, Pisa Compared with Florence, Pisa suffered little damage during the disastrous flooding of the Arno on 4 November 1966. The town stands only a few miles from the mouth of the Arno but, as with the Tiber at Ostia, silting up is always a problem.

The enchanting small church of Santa Maria della Spina, an absolute gem of Pisan Gothic architecture, was the gift to the city of a wealthy Pisan merchant. Named after a thorn from Christ's crown, it is, sadly, rarely open.

The bell of the Leaning Tower, Pisa
There is an Italian nursery rhyme which describes the Torre Pendente, saying it 'leans and leans but will never fall'. Begun in 1173, the tower was only some 10 metres high when there was a subsidence on the southern side. Building operations stopped for over a century. By 1301 the tower had reached the level of the bellchamber.

The architect, Giovanni di Simone, had tried to rectify the inclination and the tower is, in fact, slightly banana-shaped. Galileo probably used it for his experiments on the velocity of falling objects. In the 1980s the tower's rate of subsidence has been considerably decreased by pumping vast quantities of cement into the ground on the southern side.

Porta del Paradiso, Florence Lorenzo Ghiberti worked on these bronze doors from 1425 until 1452. They are on the Baptistery, facing the main portal of Florence Cathedral. Michelangelo, who was born 20 years after Ghiberti's death, called them the 'Door of Paradise'. The ten panels are being cleaned and conserved, having suffered considerable damage from the polluted atmosphere of Florence. As each panel is restored, it is placed in an hermetically-sealed display case in the Cathedral Museum. Eventually, fibre-glass models of the panels will replace the originals on the Baptistery door.

The Cathedral and the Palazzo Vecchio, Florence The existing Cathedral of Florence was built over the course of six centuries. Replacing the earlier church of Santa Maria Reparata, the Cathedral, called Santa Maria del Fiore from the lily in Florence's coat of arms, was begun in 1296. The crenellated building with the tower is the Palazzo Vecchio, the seat of the *Comune* (town council).

On Easter Sunday a great cart, bearing a large wooden edifice encircled with fireworks, is drawn round the Cathedral square by four huge white oxen before coming to rest between the main portal of the Cathedral and the Porta del Paradiso of the Baptistery. The edifice is then connected to a wire which runs back to the high altar. On the stroke of mid-day a mechanical dove begins its journey down the wire from the high altar to the edifice. When the dove strikes the firework at the top, that firework explodes and starts a chain reaction of explosions. The name of this ceremony has been quaintly translated into English as 'the Bursting of the Cart'.

Artists at work outside the Uffizi
Leonardo and Botticelli, Raphael and Titian
inside the Uffizi gallery in Florence; outside
– who knows?

**Ponte Vecchio and the Uffizi corridor,
Florence**   During their retreat from Italy
in the summer of 1944, the Germans blew
up all the bridges across the Arno save the
Ponte Vecchio. The majority of the small
wooden shops on the bridge are owned by
goldsmiths.

The corridor linking the Uffizi with the Pitti
Palace was built by Giorgio Vasari in 1565
to commemorate the marriage of
Francesco de' Medici and Joanna of Austria.

The Arno at dusk, Florence It is hard to imagine the Arno overflowing its banks and flooding so many of the low-lying quarters of Florence. The Ponte Vecchio is in the background.

Santa Croce, Florence The church of Santa Croce is Florence's equivalent of Westminster Abbey. Many of its famous sons are buried here – Michelangelo, Galileo, Macchiavelli and Gioacchino Rossini. Michelangelo's bones lie not in the dreadfully pretentious tomb designed for him by Vasari, but beneath a simple tomb slab set in the floor near Vasari's aberration.

Tuscan farmhouse near Florence Early spring in the countryside near Florence. A satisfying pattern is made by the ploughed fields and poplars.

River Adige, **Verona**   Despite *Romeo and Juliet*, despite *Two Gentlemen of Verona*, despite the summer opera season, Verona still manages to be an essentially Italian town. Many inhabitants speak the Veronese dialect and all Veronesi are as passionate in the praises of their city as are the Sienese. The town, second in size in the Veneto region only to Venice, is a centre for agricultural fairs, for conferences on education, for week-long gatherings of antiques dealers.

John Evelyn, who visited Verona in 1646, called it 'one of the delightfulest places that ever I came in'. The Veronesi keep a watchful eye on the snowfall in the Dolomites; melting snows can raise the level of the Adige which runs right through the centre of Verona.

View over Verona   To the north-east of the river Adige the land rises steeply. In the foreground of the photograph are the ruins of a second Roman theatre founded in the time of Augustus. The stone bridge – the Ponte Pietra – was blown up by the German army during its retreat in 1945. The Veronese rebuilt the bridge in its original form, dredging the Adige to salvage the Roman and mediaeval bricks and stones from which it was originally constructed. It was reopened in 1958. In the distance is Verona cathedral. The bell tower was begun in the Romanesque style, added to in the 16th century and given its bell chamber as late as 1927. In winter and early spring the melting snows of the Dolomites can turn the Adige into a raging torrent.

Performance of *Aïda*, Arena, Verona
This opera was first performed in the Arena in 1913; it met with clamorous acclaim and set new standards for spectacular opera productions. On entering the Arena each member of the audience is given a candle. These candles are lit shortly before the opera is due to begin so that performers come on to the stage to be confronted by thousands of flickering candles. In a production shortly after the Second World War, Maria Callas was so overwhelmed (she had expected a darkened auditorium) that she fainted and the performance had to be delayed until she recovered.

Piazza dei Signori and Statue of Dante, Verona   Dante fled here in 1303 to escape persecution in Florence. At that time Verona was a Ghibelline city, owing allegiance to the Emperor Henry VII. The swallow-tail crenellations of many buildings in Verona reflect this allegiance. Cities who favoured the Pope usually decorated their buildings with square crenellations. Such cities supported the Guelph faction.

Juliet's house, Verona   The 13th-century building, now much restored, was once an inn called Il Cappello, hence the connection with the Capulet family. Shakespeare obviously knew the story written about Romeo and Juliet by a 16th-century novelist called Luigi da Porto. It seems probable that the Montague (Montecchi) and Capulet (Cappello or Cappelletti) families were allies rather than enemies.

Fishing nets, Ravenna In Byzantine times Ravenna was a flourishing port as well as being the capital city of the Exarchs. Now it stands some ten kilometres from the Adriatic.

San Vitale, Ravenna The simple exterior of San Vitale belies the richness of its interior decoration – it contains some of the most impressive 6th-century mosaics in Italy. Constructed on an octagonal ground plan and built in pinkish terracotta bricks, the church was consecrated in AD 547 by Archbishop Maximian who is portrayed in the mosaic decoration of the apse. Given the wealth of mosaics in Ravenna, it is not surprising that a major foundation connected with their study and conservation has been established in the city.

Villa with lake and water-lilies, Strà Lying a little to the east of Padua, Strà is on a canalized branch of the river Brenta. The Villa Nazionale (or Pisani) is a splendid 18th-century Venetian villa which originally belonged to the Pisani family, for whom it was decorated by G.B. Tiepolo. Napoleon bought the villa from the Pisani family in 1807. It was here, in 1934, that Benito Mussolini and Adolf Hitler met for the first time.

Venice from San Giorgio Maggiore

Venice is magical; no matter how many times one visits it, no matter how long one lives there, nothing can destroy the sensation of entering an enchanted world. Perhaps it is the ever-changing light which causes one to look afresh at familiar buildings, to make new discoveries, to sit silently in some deserted *campo* in the brilliant winter sunshine, conjuring up the ghosts of Venetians dressed in the costumes painted by Guardi or Longhi.

Masked figures, Venice Carnival The *Carnevale* celebrations used to begin immediately after Christmas and continue late into the night of Shrove Tuesday. Nowadays the Carnival period lasts about two weeks, finishing on Shrove Tuesday. Venetians go about masked, some clad in magnificent costumes which they hire at a daily rate of anything up to L.200,000. Others make their own costumes, sometimes humorous (in Carnival time one can find oneself between an ostrich and a lion) — sometimes wildly imaginative.

On Shrove Tuesday Venice is thronged with crowds remarkable for their good-nature and patience. The police struggle, equally good-naturedly, to keep the revellers moving across the narrow bridges. Vast crowds can sometimes be frightening – never is it so in Carnival time in Venice. One is simply caught up in the wave of happiness and patent enjoyment.

Squero at Rio San Trovaso, Venice A boatyard where gondolas are made or repaired is called a *squero* in Italian. Nowadays a new gondola can cost as much as a medium-sized car. Long and narrow in shape, and drawing very little water, gondolas have been painted black since 1562 when a sumptuary law was passed. Before that, rival noble houses had vied with each other to have the most colourful and exotic gondolas on the canals.

Originally the gondola hull was straight from stem to stern. In the 19th century, however, it was discovered that by introducing a slight curve in the hull, the gondola could be made infinitely more manoeuvrable. It is said that the gondola can, in fact, turn on its axis.

Left A gondolier drinking wine.

San Giorgio Maggiore, Venice   Palladio's
masterpiece in Venice, the Church of San
Giorgio Maggiore, stands on the small
island of San Giorgio almost opposite the
Piazzetta di San Marco. Inside are two
resplendent late paintings by Tintoretto.

View from top of Torre dell'Orologio, Venice The clock tower, with its two figures who strike the hours, was not completed until 1496. It stands opposite the north-west corner of San Marco. At ground level its central arch marks the beginning of the Merceria, probably the most famous business street of Venice, linking as it does, the Rialto with the Piazza San Marco.

Funeral gondola, Venice The final journey for a Venetian is by water to the cemetery island of San Michele. All the emergency services in Venice use launches – police, fire and ambulance launches are the only ones allowed to exceed the speed limit in the canals.

Above A barge laden with vegetables.

Small fish market, Venice The main fish market in Venice lies on the Dorsoduro. Smaller markets can be found on many narrower canals (*rii*). The catch arrives in the very early morning and is gutted and cleaned by the time the house wives are ready to shop. Besides several varieties of flat fish, squid, octopus and eels are also in plentiful supply.

Glass-blowing, Murano The island has been the centre of the Venetian glass-blowing industry since 1292. The most beautiful artefacts date from the early years of the 16th century. Much of what is produced now is done with the tourist trade in mind. Tourists may flock to Murano; one septuagenarian islander is proud of the fact that he had once made the mile-long voyage to Venice.

Santa Maria e Donato, Murano As well as the glass-blowing factories on the island of Murano, there are two fascinating churches. One, San Pietro Martire, has a very fine altarpiece by Giovanni Bellini. The other, Santa Maria e Donato, is a gem of Ravennate Romanesque architecture. It was begun prior to AD 999, remodelled between 1125 and 1140 and has been closed for restoration since 1974. However, the exterior alone is a feast for the eye.

Between midday and 3pm the small *campo* in front of the church is deserted and two low steps make an ideal seat for peaceful contemplation of the façade.

House in Burano From Venice the steamer service calls first at the cemetery island of San Michele, then at three landing stages on Murano. Thereafter it goes to Mazzorbo which is connected by a bridge to Burano. This is a totally captivating island; the houses are painted in bright colours, the squares are immaculately clean – everything is fresh and sparkling. The lace-making school on Burano was closed in 1970 but it is still possible to see women engaged in this intricate task as they sit and gossip out of doors.

The Rialto bridge by night, Venice This bridge, built between 1588 and 1592 by Antonio da Ponte, replaced the earlier wooden one constructed in 1264. Before then, Venetians had to cross the Grand Canal by means of a bridge of boats. The word Rialto is derived from the two words *rivo alto* meaning 'high bank'. The Venetians moved their capital to this area in AD 812 after Charlemagne's son Pepin had tried unsuccessfully to capture the lagoon.

The lagoon, Venice When fog descends on Venice, a radar-controlled *vaporetto* ploughs up and down the Grand Canal, taking those who work outside Venice to the railway station or to the car park in the Piazzale Roma. When the wind blows, the waters of the lagoon can become surprisingly choppy.

Index

Acknowledgements

The Publishers would like to thank the following organisations and individuals for their kind permission to reproduce the photographs in this book:

Colorsport/Gadoffe 94–5; Susan Griggs Agency/Ted Spiegel 122; Octopus Group Picture Library/John Sims 80, 92, 106–7; Rod Panichelli 104, 104–5; Pictures Colour Library 130, 131; John Sims 86–7, 93; SPECTRUM Colour Library half-title, 10–11, 24, 26, 29, 48, 52, 54, 55, 58–9, 60, 88, 97, 126, 136 below, 140–1; /A. Allen 50; /A. Amsel 81, 84; /N. Ash 132; /D. Askham 14, 19, 40, 42, 43, 44, 102, 103, 111, 114–5, 115; /D. Ball 8–9; /Bavaria 16, 18–19, 46–7, 53, 96; /I. Booth 138; /J. Chalker 112; /G. Chapman 39; /C. Clarke 113; /T. Codrington 85, 90–1, 98; /R. Dennis 136 top; /Deva Cora 82, 83; /M. Eban 41; /Franglen 140; C. Haigh 75, 76–7, 100–1, 128–9, 135, 142; /R. Hawkins 74–5; /D & J Heaton 15, 108–9; /H. Higuchi 12; /Hulme-Sutcliffe 51; /Maj. Birch 30, 31, 49, 127; /V. Page 45; /G. Richardson 38 below, 62–3, 110–1; /V. Sharp 99; /A. R. Smith 64, 133; /R. Stutsman 12–13, 27, 28, 32; /P. Thompson title page, 56, 56–7, 61, 134–5, 139, 143; /B. Zarri 137; Judy Todd 4–5, 6, 17, 20, 21, 22–3, 25, 119; Hans Verkroost 78–9, 89.

Series editor: Alison Leach